Is This Really YOUR Day?

Is This Really YOUR Day?

◆

The Essential How—Not—To Handbook for your Engagement, Wedding, and Marriage.

Aimee Price
Illustrations by Dona Price

iUniverse, Inc.
New York Lincoln Shanghai

Is This Really YOUR Day?

The Essential How—Not—To Handbook for your Engagement, Wedding, and Marriage.

iUniverse, Inc.

For information address:
iUniverse, Inc.
2021 Pine Lake Road, Suite 100
Lincoln, NE 68512
www.iuniverse.com

ISBN: 0-595-31473-2

Printed in the United States of America

Contents

Dedication and Thanks

I dedicate this book to my loving husband Charles. The experience of our wedding has been my muse. And our wonderful marriage is a daily inspiration.

Thank you for your unconditional support and insight. You have helped guide my success. I am eternally grateful for all we share.

I also want to thank my very special illustrator, my mother. You helped capture the comical and edgy nature of my book. Your talented contribution breathed life into my words.

About the Author

Married for the second time, and having been a bridesmaid many times, Aimee Price knows from experience the utter boredom and at times discomfort of enduring yet another typical wedding. Following the traditional route with her first wedding was easy, given that her heart wasn't in it. She too made the mistake of being swept up in the event. Since then, she has become wiser for the wear. When married for the second time, knowing it was a commitment for a lifetime, she and her husband created a unique celebration that showcased their special connection. "The thought of acknowledging our vow mundanely, pained me, and was just not an option."

Aimee's experience and insight allows readers to see there are ways to make their commitment meaningful, and last a lifetime, the first time around. It doesn't take a second wedding to get it right, just some thoughtful consideration here and now.

Aimee Price currently lives in Atlanta with her husband. She is happily married and enjoying their life in the city. Aimee is currently working as a yoga instructor, and writing her second book.

Introduction

We have all attended weddings, seen them on television and in the movies, and some of us have participated in them. Stop for a moment and create an image of those matrimonial events in your mind. Surprising, isn't it? Each a different wedding, but the grandiose themes and styles are very similar.

An average of 5 million people get married in the United States each year. One would think the sheer numbers would allow for diversity, creativity, and originality within the festivities. However, all too often each celebration is a close replica of one that preceded it.

A wedding is supposed to be a day set aside to honor and commemorate the distinctive love two people share. Yet planning a wedding often becomes an all encompassing, all consuming event that takes on a life of its own. People get caught up in the whirlwind and never stop to question whether or not the routine they are following makes sense for them. Ask yourselves, if you and your partner really own this journey? What is this really all about for the two of you?

After reading this book, I am confident you and your partner will be able to incorporate some memorable and realistic alternatives to create an experience that can truly be called your own.

So, You're Engaged...

Unique Alternatives
~~~~~~~~~~~~~~~~~

Your commitment to plan a wedding together and marry one another is what makes you engaged, not a ring. A ring is nothing more than a symbol; and if that is what you are pushing for you might want to re-evaluate your motivations.

If you do exchange rings, give him an engagement ring as well. Doesn't he deserve a symbol of your commitment?

Sit down *together* and jot down what needs to be done to create the wedding you *both* want. Last time I checked, a bride *and* groom were getting married on these occasions. We need to stop making it all about the bride!

Once you know what needs to be done, divide up the responsibilities evenly. Who is going to take care of what? It is about time we abolish the "Bridezillas" and eliminate the mindless, automaton grooms.

Write your own vows. If you want your wedding day to be a unique celebration about the commitment and love the two of you share, why on earth would you say the exact same things to each other as most every other person who has married before you? Can your love really be summed up in a cookie-cutter style speech? Repeat after me, "I don't think so!"

If you have chosen to recite the traditional vows, double check the word "obey" has been eliminated. You are a woman at your wedding, not a German Shepard at obedience school! If your spouse wants someone to obey him, tell him to try the pound!

Bridal Showers, Bachelor Parties, and Bachelorette Parties...Give me a break!

Let's start with the bridal shower. This is one of the most antiquated and sexist ideas still holding fast as a tenet of tradition. Hmmm, let's see here. A bunch of ladies get together in oh so pretty floral dresses, dine on snack size foods, and watch a friend open house wares and linens. We "oohh" and "aahh" as if suddenly a crock-pot has become the most exciting thing we have ever seen. Oh Please!

Now the Bachelor Party. It is fine if the premise is a fun time out with the guys to actually celebrate the upcoming occasion. But for all you out there who still believe it is "your last night of freedom." Why the hell are you getting married in the first place? Using this event as an excuse to get hammered and dabble in illegal and illicit activities is outdated and animalistic. We wonder why the divorce rate is over 50%? Could it be the caliber of people getting married?

And finally, the Bachelorette party. Ladies, could you be more pitiful? How do you really think you look prancing around bars in a cheap veil with plastic penises attached to your clothing? You try so hard to look daring and naughty, just like your fiancé is shamefully doing at his party, but you are really quite transparent.

Let's try something different. If you want separate celebrations, guys, try a ball game, renting a fishing boat, skydiving, massages, paintball, concert, or golfing. Ladies, try a day at the spa, a Broadway show, hot air ballooning, making pottery or chocolates, a day at the beach, or museums. Or the bride and the groom can hold a "Jack and Jill" party where both people are involved, along with their closest friends, and they plan a day of activities together to celebrate the upcoming event.

When choosing the seating arrangements for your bridesmaids and groomsmen, try to remember they want to have a good time as well. Forcing them to stay artificially attached to the party member, with whom they were paired during the recessional, keeps them away from their date for the evening. Is a possibly unpleasant experience for some of your most important guests worth the image you want to create for your head table? You want to sit with your spouse, let your party members do the same.

Don't invite guests out of obligation. Invite only those with whom you actually care to celebrate. If someone gets offended, oh well, that is his or her issue. It is often said, when you try to make everyone happy, no one is happy. On your wedding, only you and your spouse need to be happy. Relish the opportunity this day gives you to be selfish.

Find a caterer willing to offer a diverse menu. We have all had the too fatty prime rib, the terribly dry chicken breast, the tad too oily salmon, or the vegetarian standard of pasta primavera. Rarely have they ever been worth raving about. The potential varieties for banquet meals are vast, tap into that resource.

We all know the bride wants to look exceptionally beautiful on her wedding day, but for those of you who choose to do so at the expense of your bridesmaid's dignity, think again. When choosing wedding attire for your nearest and dearest friends, choose class and elegance over taffeta and ruffles. You will not be upstaged if your bridal party looks beautiful. Instead, their stunning presentation will further compliment yours. When brides choose tacky attire with the hopes of looking the best, everyone just pities the bridesmaids and believes you have no taste.

If you register for gifts, make sure there are plenty of price options. Not every person can afford to buy the China or crystal, nor should they have to. You may choose to go into debt for your wedding, but it should not be a prerequisite for your guests.

We all know some temporary debt may be acquired after planning a wedding. However, the key here is *temporary* debt! If you can't afford to pay it off ASAP, you can't afford to have it at all. The burden of unnecessary debt can be devastating to the stability of a marriage. The price of your perfect wedding should not cost you your marriage.

When deciding on favors, keep your guests in mind. I am sure everyone attending cares for both of you, but do they really want something engraved with your monogram or names? How about a picture of the happy couple? Not unless it is for your mother. Instead give them something they can actually enjoy: a potted plant, chocolates, candles, or lottery tickets.

Hanging in There…

Pause to Ponder
~~~~~~~~~~~~~~

Ask yourselves, "Why do I want to spend the rest of my life with this person?" Pretend, "being in love" is not an acceptable answer. What else is there?

Top three reasons for divorce: Disputes over Money, Children, and In-Laws. How are you going to handle each of these issues to help protect your marriage? Have a no-holds-barred discussion. Speak your mind; own your voice! If you conflict over these issues, negotiate a compromise with which you are both happy.

The intention of marriage is eternity. But we all have our limits: adultery, abuse, addictions, etc. What would absolutely make you call it quits? Share these thoughts with your partner. Now ask yourself if you can live within or to those standards and expectations.

Make a list of all the wonderful aspects of your relationship. Share this list with your partner. Now make a list of all the things you would like to see improve, but keep the statements positive. For example, instead of, "We yell when we fight." Try, "We could learn to settle disagreements calmly." Share this list with your partner. Where do you agree? Where do you disagree? Negotiate a compromise for items in disagreement.

Ask yourself if you can be truly intimate with your partner. Can you comfortably and safely share with him/her all the little details about who you are, that you keep tucked away from the rest of the world? If not, why are you choosing to spend the rest of your life with this person? If so, you are one step closer to a successful union.

The Wedding Is Here...

A New Twist on Tradition

~~~~~~~~~~~~~~~~~~~

Walk down the aisle alone or consider walking down together. The traditional method was designed under the premise of the daughter as property, moving from the ownership of her father to the ownership of her husband. Aren't you more independent than that?

"Here comes the bride…" You don't say! Who else would it be? But thank you for stating the obvious. Now, whichever way you finally choose to walk down the aisle, choose another song than that.

Make sure the official performing the ceremony knows the two of you well enough to personalize the ceremony. Reading verbatim from the scripture, minimal eye contact, offering thoughts to the congregation identical to those at each wedding prior to yours...oh the poignancy and genuine sentiment just bring me to tears. Doubtful! This is the only day the two of you will become husband and wife, put a little heart into it for goodness sake.

People spend a lot of time choosing the perfect music for their reception and often neglect the music for the ceremony. The ceremony is, after all, the point of the entire day and thus deserves to be complimented as such. If you choose to use a musician available to you through the ceremony site, please make sure they are actually talented. There is nothing worse than sitting through a ceremony constantly interrupted by a tone-deaf organist or someone worthy of a cheesy lounge act in Vegas.

Forget the receiving line. It is impersonal and awkward. Why on earth does every guest have to shake the hand of Billy the Groomsmen and Dana the Bridesmaid? We don't know them, and we certainly aren't going to get to know them during that two-minute superficial interaction. Find a more creative and personal way to thank your guests.

At your reception, mix the event up a bit. Rather than:

- Introduction as husband and wife

- Couple dance

- Wedding party joins

- Father/daughter dance

And on and on it drones…Try being more creative. Be in the reception hall before all the guests and welcome them inside. Dance at unexpected times. Just take the typical, traditional routine and eliminate it from your repertoire. Your guests will appreciate the unanticipated lightheartedness, and it will help keep you in the moment.

Tell your photographer you both worked really hard to make this day special and you want to enjoy it completely. So, they need to work for their money and find a way to take photographs without being intrusive and without pulling you away from your much planned for and anticipated event.

It is more poignant for the photographer to actually capture the event, as opposed to just how everyone looked. Heads tilted, stiff smiles...the resemblance to mannequins is uncanny. Try a candid approach. The unexpected surprise of emotions frozen in time can be breathtaking.

Tell your videographer to get that awfully bright light out of your guests' faces.

Tell your videographer not to interview your guests on tape. What a waste of film and money! Do you really need to pay thousands to have some stranger hold up a camera to your guests to hear each one say, "Congratulations. We're happy for you—best of luck. When are you having children?" Ask him/her to be more ingenious than that and actually capture the essence of the event.

Please, oh please, leave the inflatable toys for the sweet sixteen parties. If your DJ or band attempts to bring them out, pop them! They are tacky.

The *YMCA* and *Chicken Dance*? It is not the Eighties anymore. Enough said.

Make sure your musical performers entertain at a noise level that enhances the event, and allows guests to still converse. Louder is not better—just deafening.

Grab your new spouse and kiss him/her randomly throughout the night. But please don't kiss on command when the glasses clink. Do you normally perform on command? Instead, start clinking your glass as well and soon everyone will see just how silly it is.

Make sure your caterer knows who is to be served what at each table. It is terribly distasteful to turn your dinner reception into an auction as the servers walk around yelling, "Who had the prime rib?"

Before you do the customary bouquet toss, know which single women are in attendance. There is no sense in embarrassing the poor 30-something soul who is single among a bunch of teenagers. Instead, offer the bouquet to a happily engaged couple, since it symbolizes the next to marry.

Keep your garter on your leg and leave it there for only your husband to see. Is your wedding reception really the place to have your skirt hiked up? It is supposed to be an elegant affair after all.

Try being more creative with your dessert choice. Sure a cake can look beautiful, but they cost an awful lot and often don't taste the most decadent. The dessert at your wedding should be *melt-in-your-mouth* sinful. Instead, find your favorite bakery and offer a variety of cakes, cookies, pastries, and/or chocolates. Have one large plate of bite-size treats set up for each table. I am sure your guests would enjoy a plate filled with delectable little samplings of some of the finer desserts, as opposed to a sliver of yellow cake with butter cream icing.

Eat and drink. You spent a lot of money and time meticulously choosing the menu; enjoy it! Don't set yourself up for failure by preprogramming your brain with the message, "I will be too nervous to eat." Nervous about what? You just married the love of your life? If that isn't a celebration to enjoy some great food and drink, I don't know what is.

You're Married, Now What...?

After the Glitz and Glam

~~~~~~~~~~~~~~~~~~~~

The absolute best way to get what you want from your partner is to give them what they want. Find out your partner's needs and desires and meet them. Do you see what a beautiful cyclical effect this will have if you are both always doing this?

Love your partner each day as if it were the last day you had the opportunity to do so. In all reality, it just might be.

Keep your private moments private. Don't gossip with the girls or laugh it up with guys, at your partner's expense. Those private moments, large and small, are what help make your relationship truly unique to the two of you. Cherish them.

If you want your partner to be your best friend, treat them that way. Talk with each other, laugh together, do things for fun.

Disagree with dignity. Do not disrespect or degrade each other during disputes. Such damage is difficult to undo.

Resolve disputes promptly. You might have to agree to disagree, but life is too short to waste time with grudges or brewing anger.

People have often said history repeats itself. Don't allow this to become the mantra of your arguments. If you have a disagreement, keep it in the present and stay focused. **Do Not** bring up previous infractions. Keep the past history!

Pick Your Battles!!! I cannot emphasize this enough! In the grand scheme of life, who really cares if a dirty sock is left on the floor or the garbage got too full. Get over it!

Never play the, "What's wrong Honey? ~ Nothing, game." If something is wrong, you own those feelings and you should do so proudly. Maybe you need some time to cool off, fine, but then speak when you are ready, with confidence and conviction. But don't play games! They are really annoying.

Do lots of little things for each other. Leave unexpected happy notes for your partner. Say, "I love you" when they least expect it.

Make your hugs count. Embrace long enough until you feel just a little more relaxed because of it.

Don't neglect sex, but don't schedule it either. Enjoy each other's bodies, just for the sake of appreciating their beauty. Kiss, caress, massage, nibble, tickle, but don't always let it lead to sex. Keep the arousal high and the senses stimulated, and sex will happen often and naturally enough.

When you are wrong, admit it. It is more liberating than one would think and it eliminates unnecessary confrontations.

Hold hands.

Do not ask the question, if you aren't prepared to accept the honest answer. Before you ask potentially volatile questions, ask yourself if the answer is, one, something you must know, and, two, something you can accept regardless of its nature. Remember, if honesty is something you cultivate within your relationship, then you cannot make exceptions when the honest answer to a potentially leading question may be unpleasant.

Your way isn't necessarily the right way. Continually be open to different possibilities and perspectives. This helps keep life and marriage new and refreshing.

You took a vow to commit yourself to your partner for a lifetime, do everything in your power to honestly uphold that promise. Treasure the wonderful moments, learn from the hardships, and love each other through it all.

0-595-31473-2